TERRIFYING ORDEAL

by

Paul Birtill

Hearing Eye

ACKNOWLEDGEMENTS

First published March 1998
Second edition December 1998

This publication has been made possible with the financial assistance of the London Arts Board.

Printed by Aldgate Press, London E1
Typesetting by Copyart, London NW5
Cover design concept by Paul Rasmussen

ISBN 1 870841 55 7

Some of these poems first appeared in the following places:

The Guardian, The Independent, The New Statesman, Outposts, Acumen, The Rialto, Envoi, Poetry Nottingham, Spokes, The Echo Room, Scratch, The Frogmore Papers, Pennine Platform, Psychopoetica, Braquemard, Gargoyle, Brixton Poets, Tops, Shrike, Rising, Out From Beneath The Boot, Poems on the London Buses, Poems on the Internet, BBC Radio Merseyside.

A Selection of Poems from Terrifying Ordeal were published by *Hearing Eye*. in 1996, reprinted 1997.

With thanks to: Paul Rasmussen, Grant Fraser, Martyn Watts, Mary Reid.

****

to my dead parents...

****

Published by Hearing Eye, Box 1, 99 Torriano Avenue, London NW5 2RX

CONTENTS

KEEPING WATCH 5
79 KINGFIELD 6
PROBLEMS DESCRIBING
A DEAD PERSON 7
CHRISTMAS IN BEDSIT LAND 7
CHEATING DEATH 8
GETTING TO SEVENTY 8
WAITING FOR MY MOTHER 9
COUPLES 9
OUT WALKING WITH MY FATHER 10
OBSESSIVE THINKER 11
WILL I BE ABLE TO DIE 12
LONER 12
SAD BASTARD 13
STRANGERS ON A TUBE 14
THE MAN WHO COULDN'T CHANGE 14
ONLY THE APPALLING DIE OLD 14
BITTER OLD FART 15
THE SHED 16
BODY TALK 17
REINCARNATION 18
NERVOUS TWITCH 18
FATHER-IN-LAW 19
VEGETARIAN 19
ME TOO 19
GETTING THROUGH 20
LOVE 20
LOVE AT FIRST SIGHT 21
BABIES AND BEARDS 21
AFFECTION 21
THE HAIRCUT 22
STINKIN' PARTY 23
GOD WORKS IN MYSTERIOUS WAYS 24
GIVE ME A BOY AT AN IMPRESSIONABLE AGE 25
PRIEST WITHOUT A HEAD 26
TRAGIC SMELL 26
LOVED AND SLAUGHTERED 27
WAKING UP 28
THE UNKNOWN GLASS COLLECTOR 28
NEUROSIS 29
ALTON'S AMENDMENT 30
JILTED 31
SO MANY WAYS TO DIE 31
FALLING IN SHIT 32
WORK-SHY WRITER 33
SMOKING IN BED 33
TERRIFYING ORDEAL 34
FEMINIST 35
AIM LOW SCORE HIGH 35
PESTERING THE DOCTOR 36

DATING 36
THOUGHT FOR THE DAY 37
BAD BACK 37
CHEER UP 38
TWO SHORT LOVE POEMS:
LAZY & BETTER 38
WANKING 39
ALARM CALL 40
MAD COW 40
IAN BOTHAM'S UNDERPANTS 41
SCRATCHED CAR 42
MEN AND MOTHERS 42
ME OR THEM 43
FOR TED HUGHES 43
CONVERSATION 43
NEVER TIRING 44
SHOULD HAVE GUESSED 44
SLEEPING AROUND 45
JUST HAD TO KNOW 45
EYEWITNESS 46
DISTURBED 46
ILL AT EASE 46
NOT CELEBRATING THE NEW DECADE 47
TO ME 48
TALKING IN BOXES 49
EARLY IMPRESSIONS 49
THE GREAT HUMAN FARCE 50
STRIVING FOR IMPERFECTION 50
DIFFERENT KIND OF FATHER 51
STONE THROWING 51
PAUL 52
WIND UP 52
MY DOCTOR 52
PATRIOTIC WHITE YOUTH 53
DEATH 54
THE SECRET CRIER 55
HORRIBLE THOUGHT 55
NO SECONDS NO AFTERS 56
C2 H5 OH 56
HYPOCRITE 57
MIRROR 57
EXPOSED 57
BRILLIANT STUDENT 58
MAN TO MAN 59
G.B.H. 59
THE LAVATORY ATTENDANT 60
UNHAPPY HOUR 61
NATURE POEM 61
FIREMEN 62
THE LONELY RASPBERRY BLOWER 63
GAMES WITH GRANMA 63
HURRY UP AND DIE 64
BEST SELLER 64
SUDDEN REALISATION 64

KEEPING WATCH

There is a history of insanity
in that family going back three
generations and they watch each
other like hawks for signs.
They are over-controlled in that house
impulsive behaviour is non-existent.
I stayed there once and nobody
laughed shouted sang cried or
did anything emotional they just
watched - they watched each other
like hawks for signs and
one said as I was leaving,
"It's in our genes you know..."

79 KINGFIELD

There wasn't much room
in our house so I crashed
in Ma's room 'til I was ten.

Sometimes she'd get up and
piss in an orange bucket
Quite often she'd see something
and call out
I hated the night...

Occasionally the old man
would creep in, tip-toe
past my bed and give
her one, unaware I was
awake listening.
They were both in their fifties
I hated the night...

She became ill and
moaned with pain
throughout the night
getting up to take
pills walk about
and piss in the orange bucket.
The old man stopped coming...

When I was ten my
dad built an attic on
the roof and I got my own room
small though it was
the nights were peaceful,
I learnt to sleep...

PROBLEMS DESCRIBING A DEAD PERSON

The argument was about
whether or not LOVING FATHER
should be inscribed on his
tomb and it raged for three
days and three nights with
short breaks for food. Many
a violent word was spoken
and at one point Fred said
he'd smash the grave with
a hammer. It was finally
resolved by a sensitive
neighbour who came up
with an acceptable compromise
SADLY MISSED BY SOME

CHRISTMAS IN BEDSIT LAND

Christmas is coming
and there's a violent maniac
in the attic.
He keeps threatening to
come down and give me a
good hiding because I have
lots of callers and he has none.
I've told the landlady but
she sez she can't evict him
until he actually gives me
the hiding.
He sez he's gonna do it
right after the Queen's speech
and I believe him...

CHEATING DEATH

No ambulance siren
No audience or crowd
No morbid doctor with
shocking diagnosis
No months of pain
and messing the bed
No operating theatres
or cream painted wards
just two hundred tranquillisers
and a room by the sea
Oh yes it's Hastings for me...

GETTING TO SEVENTY

I haven't got the skills
friends or family to take
me up to seventy.
I haven't got the will
qualifications or necessary
experience to take me
up to seventy.
I haven't got the health
stamina or special
relationship to take
me up to seventy.
I might make fifty though...

WAITING FOR MY MOTHER

Fifty-three and totally grey
Wishing to avoid the
young mothers - was always
        last to arrive.
I could wait twenty minutes
and then, when the road was clear
in an old coat, looking tired
        and perhaps
        a little embarrassed
        She'd appear.
I was always pleased to
see her - well worth
waiting for was my old mum.

COUPLES

Couples are a nuisance
they're always waiting
for you to leave so they
can start mauling one another.
There's only me and this
fat kid with glasses left
in the village who haven't
got a girlfriend and he's
asked me to go on holiday;
everybody's watching us.

OUT WALKING WITH MY FATHER

That woman's got
cancer of the hand
it may spread
it may not.
That building's not safe
it's going to collapse
and kill people -
little children probably.
A man strangled
a woman in that
park last year.
That dog could
bite you and
give you rabies.
Watch a car
doesn't hit you
or you'll end up
with no legs.
Out walking with my father
the world became a terrifying place...

OBSESSIVE THINKER

He doesn't go to work
just lies on his bed
and thinks
He reads no books and
writes no letters
just lies on his bed
and thinks
In fact he has no hobbies
or interests except that
is to think
He doesn't drink in company
prefers to drink and think.
He eats TV dinners - they're
quick an' easy to prepare
which means more time
to think
He never goes to sleep at night
just lies there and thinks
And what does he think about?
Whether or not he's having a good time.....

WILL I BE ABLE TO DIE

Will I be able
to die
Do I have
what it takes
Do I have
the guts
Will I be able
to relax enough
when the time comes
- let go completely
or might I chicken
out at the last moment
and will the doctor
have to smother me with
a pillow - how humiliating...

LONER

He was so used to his own company
that whenever anyone
spoke to him - asked
him his name or how
he was feeling - assumed
for a moment he had just
been in a road accident and
they were trying to keep him alive...

SAD BASTARD

Wears shades to
hide the pain
health irrelevant
appearance unimportant
happiness not recalled
No-one likes a sad bastard...

Alone in a pub
not looking around
not interested
quite still
life's a chore
No-one likes a sad bastard...

Snivelling in a bedsit
eating beans from a can
ripping up suicide notes
watching a kids programme
No-one likes a sad bastard...

Shuffling through a park
having bitter thoughts
chucks stones at the ducks
shouts abuse at a squirrel
lies in the wet grass and cries
No-one wants a sad bastard...

Passes the Samaritans
on his way home
gives it two fingers
and starts to run
A sudden flash of courage
- he can do it,
this time it's for real
who'll miss a sad bastard...

STRANGERS ON A TUBE

He picked his nose
She laughed
He wiped it on her coat
She slapped his face
He head-butted her
I carried on reading Keats -
- thank God for poems on the Underground...

THE MAN WHO COULDN'T CHANGE

He watched his sister change
many times during her breakdown
so equated it with madness
and like a dead tree - for
fifteen years forced himself
to stay, and be, exactly the
same; in case they should send
him to the asylum too.

ONLY THE APPALLING DIE OLD

Do you have a nasty
little plan to get
you through your
horrible span.

How many people
will you destroy
to bring about
your pride and joy.

And will you have
the cheek to say
there simply was
no other way...

BITTER OLD FART

I didn’t smoke
and now I’m deaf...

didn’t drink
now I’m incontinent

didn’t have late nights
now I’m senile...

didn’t eat junk food
yet I can hardly see...

didn’t take drugs
yet I ache all over...

didn’t laze about
yet I’m stuck in this chair...

didn’t get fat
now I’ve shrunk...

didn’t take risks
now I stink the
place out...

didn’t overspend
now I’m poor...

I never really enjoyed myself
like other people but they’re
all dead, and I’m alone...

THE SHED

I watched the new tenants
pull down the old shed on Sunday afternoon
and remembered the day it was first
erected, some twenty years ago.
It took half an hour to dismantle
yet had taken the Gunnings two
sons, Francis and Arthur most of
an afternoon to build. Their parents
who were on holiday at the time
had been pestering them to put one
up for months, and I think it was
meant as a surprise. When they
had finished they began to argue
and then fight. I shouted
at them both to stop as they rolled around
the lawn exchanging blows and screaming
at one another, but they took no notice.
Then Arthur grabbed a hammer and walloped
Francis several times over the head with it
- he later died in hospital. The Gunnings
returned home the next day to discover they'd
gained a shed and lost a son...

BODY TALK

I hate my body
and it hates me
I fill it with tar
and tons of ale
it responds with
horrible pains
We have no respect
for one another
we give each other hell...

I exercise it rarely
and feed it some
awful shit it
retaliates with more
horrible pains
What a carry on...

Soon we'll part company
and the fighting will end
but not before it puts
me through agony for the
years I've mistreated it
horrible bloody thing...

REINCARNATION

Is this ladybird
Sir Oswald Mosley
Is this cockroach
Sir Stafford Cripps
Is this beetle
Pitt the younger
Is my cat Heydrich
'the hangman'
I'll boot its arse
just in case...

NERVOUS TWITCH

Can you imagine anything more unfashionable than an uncontrollable nervous twitch like shaking your head or blinking your eyes for instance. I often wonder about twitches and how disastrous it would be to develop one. I sit in my executive chair and shudder at the thought of shaking my head down at the club or screwing up my face hideously at a dinner party - I'd lose all my social status in one twitch. I might even become an outcast if it got bad enough - a laughing stock for sure. Sometimes I stand in front of the mirror do a few little twitches and then run to the drinks cabinet and pour myself a large whisky.

FATHER-IN-LAW

He didn't like the mechanic
who wanted the daughter he
fancied but after a fight
gave her away. They moved
next door and now both men
enjoy a pint together on
Sundays, talk about sex and
work under the car...

VEGETARIAN

I wish I was a vegetarian
Sometimes then I could
boil a potato and eat it
with a stupid smile on my face ...

ME TOO

Some of these poets
have big ideas especially
after they've had a few beers
- imagine they'll be read
in a hundred years...!

GETTING THROUGH

Struggling striving surviving
but for what?
So you can die
So you can say
you got through
but to who?
those fellow sufferers
merely getting through.
You're punishing yourself
for nothing and the dead
are laughing at you...

LOVE

Those who need love the least
get the most and those who
need it the most often get
none at all.

The happy get happier
while the sad get sadder
- cruel state of affairs...

LOVE AT FIRST SIGHT

Girl meets washing machine
Spin dryer, dishwasher, fridgedaire
three piece suite, colour telly
body guard, handyman entertainer
Sperm bank, back hander large garden
foreign holiday, chauffeur microwave
persian carpet, loft conversion
electrical appliance bit of jewellery
widow's pension..

BABIES AND BEARDS

Women must have kids
- try it at least once
as men do with beards.
But beards don't cause
wars poverty and unhappiness...

AFFECTION

Couldn't show it
Didn't know it
Thought it was
a diseased condition.
Such a shame
No-one to blame...

THE HAIRCUT

How are you?
Alright.
What'll it be?
The usual.
What's that?
Don't you remember?
No.
You just asked me how I was.
(PAUSE)
Don't you remember me?
No I'm afraid not.
Do you remember this lump
on the back of my neck?
Oh yes I remember that.
The usual is it?
Yes and make sure
the hair covers it...

STINKIN' PARTY

Flirting with an assortment of sheer rubbish
exchanging lines with smiling enthusiasts
thirsting for dialogue.
A hundred or so bloody good moods
crammed into a noisy little room.
Half dancing rotating heads scouting
for a spouse to spend half a century with.
Excited enough to wet your pants like a
dog that's been chained up for a week.
Burying one's liquor in the garden to
ensure drunkenness throughout.

Bell warns of new arrivals with fresh dialogue.
But why should I converse with these keen
sparkling hyped up shit-bags who've been
ignoring me on the underground all week.
Giving them the attention reserved for dying relatives
they'll not get a peep out of me.

Wish I was the gate-crasher who treads
dog muck into every carpet, nicks a few ornaments,
- fucks off early.

Those with style, superior lines and an
above average jig end up in a room fit
for pigs spending the remainder of the
night rolling round a cold floor
touching up several stone of unfamiliar
foul smelling flesh.

They take it to a bit of green
the next day, clutch its grubby
hand like they've known it for years -
make arrangements for a weekend by the sea.

Eighty per cent of accidents
occur in the home, why can't
we see a few at parties...

GOD WORKS IN MYSTERIOUS WAYS

Aberfan, Multiple Sclerosis
Spastics and the Somme
Bloody Mysterious...

Cancer, Culloden
Famine and President Botha
Weird...

Motorway pile-ups
Cot-deaths and Hiroshima
A trifle peculiar...

Schizophrenia, Zeebrugge
Thatcherism and Belsen
Damn strange...

Aids and Ulster
Strokes, Cardboard City
and of course the
human being

Is he worth an hour
on Sunday?
Surely not...

GIVE ME A BOY AT AN IMPRESSIONABLE AGE

I dance
like a Roman Catholic

Almost no movement...

I stare at women's breasts
like a Roman Catholic

Barely a glance...

I talk about sex
like a Roman Catholic

A couple of lines when I'm pissed...

I hug like a Roman Catholic
when seeing someone off on a journey
(Only)

I make love
like a Roman Catholic

In the dark ashamed...

I'm drinking myself to death

(and I'm not even a Roman Catholic)

PRIEST WITHOUT A HEAD

When I was a child
I used to dream a lot
of headless priests
coming towards me in
their silk vestments -
arms stretched out.
My dad told me seeing
the priest without a
head meant that I would
lose my faith as an adult.
Some years later our parish
priest lost his head in a car crash...

TRAGIC SMELL

The whisky
on your breath
smells horrible.
It smells of domestic
violence deprived children
and good friends lost forever.

The whisky
on your breath
is making me sick.
It smells of corruption
in low places the theft
of fifteen pounds a cheap
affair and losing at the races.

The smell of whisky on your breath
makes me quite depressed...

LOVED AND SLAUGHTERED

Better to have loved and lost
than never to have experienced rejection.

Better to have loved and lost
than never to have suffered
humiliation and pain.

Better to have loved and lost
than never to have felt
jealousy and hate.

Better to have loved and lost
than never to have known
such despair.

Better to have loved and lost
than never to have felt
like a total ass.

Better to have loved
and lost than never
to have swallowed
a bottle of pills.

Better to have loved
and lost than never
to have kept your
pride and dignity.

Better to have loved
and lost than never
to have lost at all...

WAKING UP

Last night I dreamt
I was a child again
playing by a stream.

Last night I dreamt
I was on holiday and
fell in love.

Last night I dreamt
it was my twenty-first
birthday and I was very
drunk.

This morning I awoke in
my hospital bed remembered
I was dying and cried..

THE UNKNOWN GLASS COLLECTOR

There was an old glass collector
in Maida Vale who often pestered
me whilst I drank my ale.
He boasted many friends -
I thought he must be sound
Yet he was dead four weeks
before his body was found...

NEUROSIS

Being tense a way of life
as happy as your phobias allow
A cripple without a wheelchair...

Frightened to live
frightened to die
Alcohol, fags - valium nearby...

No peace of mind
a conflict with self
Shrinks, bad dreams
Palpitations and dizzy spells...

Obsessional behaviour
the order of the day
A twitch here
a twitch there
touching this
touching that
Compulsive thoughts
you'd rather not have...

Only half living
in a kind of purgatory
with contorted face
and bleak outlook
sympathy from no-one
no chance of a cure...

ALTON'S AMENDMENT

Measles, the stick
exams and acne
bullying at the dentist
prefer to have my spine bust.

Unemployment or mundane tasks
broken hearts and shattered
dreams, accidents rape, worrying
to an ulcer, tranquillisers or
booze? break my spine instead.

Middle-aged failure,
depressed wasted debts,
boredom and balding.
Sooner have my head crushed.

Diseases, senility
operations and loneliness
mugged for tuppence.
No more praying
it's nearly over now
just some agonising pain
and the nightmare ends.

Hope no stinkin' couple
disturbs my sleep again...

JILTED

She said I was a bore
and took off with a stevedore
She said I was dull
and when I did talk
it was mostly bull
She said I was ineffective in bed
and suspected weird things
went on in my head
She said I lacked bite
and couldn't imagine me
winning a fight
She said I'd be no good
as a dad
- that all her kids would
turn out mad
She said we were an
incorrect match
and I was an incredibly
shitty catch...

SO MANY WAYS TO DIE

So obsessed with death
in all its forms - he
wanted to die not once,
but a thousand times -
trying every single cause
of death known to man.
How frustrating he thought
that a person could only
die of one ailment. However
he was comforted by the fact
there may be complications...

FALLING IN SHIT

A certain smile
or silly look
An accent or a laugh
some hackneyed phrase
or witty one liner
I'm falling in shit...

A piece of cabbage
between the teeth
A raincoat soaked through
tripping in the street
dropping an ice cream
nearly choking on a fishbone
I'm falling in shit...

A cut finger
some burnt sausages
An unusual gift
a thoughtful gesture
A birthmark, plaster
pattern on a jumper
I'm falling in shit...

Some angry exchanges
a button coming off a shirt
a sad tale
A bit of eccentricity
a minimum of defects
- possibly going places
I've fallen in shit...

WORK-SHY WRITER

You get lazy people
in any field, I write poems
instead of novels. You start
at nine and finish at half
past and have the rest of
the day to yourself - money's
crap though...

SMOKING IN BED

I always have a cigarette
last thing
I turn out the light
lie back and spark up
I love to smoke in bed...

Often I wake up
with my quilt on fire
or the ashtray over my head
There are holes in my
Pillow and sheets
but I love to smoke
in bed...

One day the whole
house will go up
and there are kiddies
in the flat above
But I don't give
a monkey's
I love to smoke
in bed...

TERRIFYING ORDEAL

Sex is smelly
sex is bad
messy and 'orrible
not in my pad...

Hate the word
loathe the effort
diseases brats
and raised blood pressure...

Clumsily in the dark
we fiddle about
a pathetic attempt at affection
about as relaxing as having a tooth pulled...

Embarrassing pointless
overrated nonsense.
A time consuming
unhygienic farce
enjoyed by shit-heads...

A competitive complicated
recurring nuisance
an absurd form of communication
favoured by pea brains...

Wipe my arse
and I'll wipe yours
but no more please
nothing about you turns
me on except the cancer-
growth I suspect blossoms
in your breast...

FEMINIST

If I were a feminist
I should prefer a
bible-thumping misogynist
to a liberated male
who changes one in
ten nappies and lets
me go to my night-class
on Thursdays...

AIM LOW SCORE HIGH

Whilst trying
to emulate Jesus Christ
I lost all my friends
and got my head kicked
in four times.
My mate on the other hand
who was inspired by King
Herod in his early teens
seems to be having a ball
of a time - everybody loves him.
I might have a crack at Bonaparte
when I leave hospital...

PESTERING THE DOCTOR

I rang my doctor this morning
and asked him if wearing tight
jeans would aggravate my sciatica.
He told me he had people dying
of cancer in his surgery and hung up.
So I rang him back and asked would
it be safe to re-heat a steak 'n' kidney
pie from yesterday...

DATING

I always give a heil Hitler salute
on my first date and rant on about
badger baiting.
I never show my good side,
they always bugger off.

Sometimes I smack myself in the face,
refuse to buy a round, or talk about
life in a mental hospital.
I never show my good side,
they always bugger off.

But usually I just get steaming drunk
and talk of human scum - this one never
fails to alienate and send them on the run...

THOUGHT FOR THE DAY

I wish for once the
day would not begin
the night is not long
enough - it seems no time
at all and the birds start
their bloody twittering and
we're off again...

BAD BACK

Can't bend
Can't lift
Can't slouch
Unsexy uncool
Can't sit on a
Bleedin' stool
Girls hate a bad back...

Doesn't show on X-ray
Difficult to prove
Work-shy dole cheat
Malingering fraud
The State hate a bad back...

Difficult to treat
Impossible to cure.
A baffling mystery
A nuisance an' a bore
Doctor's hate a bad back...

CHEER UP

Sometimes when I'm
feeling a bit low
I imagine I'm out
walking in the
New Forest, about
to tread on an adder...

TWO SHORT LOVE POEMS

LAZY

How can I fall in love
I can't even muster the
energy to clean out the toilet...

BETTER

Better to have loved and lost
than to have lived in a caravan

WANKING

The best value for
money I know
An unstressful private
business hurting no other.

Anytime, anywhere
this simple act can
be enjoyed by young
and old alike.

Imagination ensures
a good time
Magazines videos
and binoculars
for the less inspired.

The oldest thrill
known to man
Enjoyed by Moses
written about by
the apostles.

Five minutes a day
keeps frustration
at bay
A bit of handwork
a box of tissues
and you're away.

Wanking!
for the way you live
your life today...

ALARM CALL

When I was eighteen
still living at home
I was awoken each morning
by the screams of a then
undiagnosed schizophrenic.
She'd run upstairs bang
on my door and ask me
what I wanted for my birthday.
Sometimes she'd ask me when
I thought I might die and go
away laughing.
My sister now lives on her own by the sea
and I have an alarm clock...

MAD COW

She's a mad cow
suffering from mad cow disease
and the mad cow is going to die
because there's no cure - so die
cow die, die you mad cow...

IAN BOTHAM'S UNDERPANTS

Stylish career women
spin round in minis
and have nicer legs than nurses...

Hard and cold
like their men tough, but sane
Never progressing from the wendy-house
only looks keep them out the gutter...

Spirited face-slappers
G-strings with spending power
disguising their common origins
Seducing Alsatian dogs...

Normally blonde, quite often
stupid, always Tory.
Union Jacks and make-up
Prawn cocktails in Spain...

Secretly loathing the tattooed
muscles they cuddle each night
too thick to be lesbian
prefer watching Cave-men scrap...

Haters of the Wimp
intolerant of the Weirdo
inspired by the crook
Prepared to fight tooth and nail
for a pair of Botham's undies.

SCRATCHED CAR

Before terminating our friendship
he gave me a lecture.
I had to listen
he held the moral high ground
I scratched his car you see;
used my keys and went right
around forming a circle almost.
I offered him a pair of scissors
and told him to cut the arm of
my new leather jacket but he
declined and continued with
his lecture - verbal psychopath...

MEN AND MOTHERS

Fussing cuddling
ironing my short pants
I can handle this jungle
Cos mum's about...

And when I get older
and mummy is dead
I'll find a substitute
to pat my head...

She'll not be like mum
but will have a nice bum
she'll fail all mum's tests
but will have nice breasts...

If she's disloyal, unlike Ma'mar
I'll get stinking in my local bar.
Then back home I'll throw a fit,
and knock the wench about a bit...

ME OR THEM

Is it me
or is it them
Is it me
or is it them
Is it me
or is it them
Why do I live
on my own
Is it me
or is it them...

FOR TED HUGHES

The birds are migrating
- who gives a fuck ...

CONVERSATION

Fact
joke
interruption
lie
silence
fact
pause
insult
rubbish
half truth
exaggeration
mug's game

NEVER TIRING

I wish I could
live a hundred times
in a hundred different places
as a hundred different people
a hundred years a piece ...

SHOULD HAVE GUESSED

I always wondered
about you.
I should have guessed
really it was obvious.
Even at school I suppose
the signs were there,
and then afterwards when
you avoided everyone,
Why didn't I realise
you were in the Knights
of St Columba...

SLEEPING AROUND

Sleeping around
Sleeping around
What is all this
Sleeping around

Sleeping around
Sleeping around
Where is all this
Sleeping around

Sleeping around
Sleeping around
Why is there all this
Sleeping around

Sleeping around
Sleeping around
Who's doing all this
Sleeping around...

JUST HAD TO KNOW

Obsessed with the idea of an afterlife
climbed out onto his tenth floor balcony
and shouted 'In ten seconds I'll know
the answer to the question we've all
wondered about since time began.' But
as he went to jump caught his foot
in the rail and was left dangling
over the edge for half an hour,
eventually dropping into a large
blanket which the laughing crowd
held out...

EYEWITNESS

Yesterday I witnessed
something quite strange.
My next door neighbour
a Jehovah's witness stole
a pint of milk from my
doorstep and drank it in
his garden laughing...

DISTURBED

A fire rages in my mind
- the inescapable torture
of an unresolved unforgiving
past that returns to haunt me.
Time does not and cannot heal
this festering wound which does
not abate and only a death, without
an afterlife to still remember will
kill this mortal flame of torment...

ILL AT EASE

I've always felt
uncomfortable on this planet
never quite at ease
forever looking over my shoulder
or checking my pulse
I don't know what it is
really but I just can't
get comfortable...

NOT CELEBRATING THE NEW DECADE

Didn't care to celebrate
maybe falling down the stairs
electrocuting myself losing
one or both parents getting
hit by a car - having my first operation
No hugs for me at twelve o'clock
I sat in a dark room biting my nails...

Didn't care to celebrate my
relationship ending nastily
my hair falling out getting
into debt some form of mental
illness my first suicide attempt
another world war
No hugs for me at twelve o'clock
I sat in a dark room shaking
uncontrollably...

Didn't care to celebrate
losing my job getting
butted in a bar ominous pains
in my left arm and not prepared
to revel in future misfortunes
sat chain smoking in a dark room
No hugs for me at twelve o'clock...

TO ME

He did this to me
to me to me
he did it to me
He hit me - me me
he hit me

She was rude to me
to me - was rude to me
She jilted me
Me jilted me

He stole off me
Me me he stole
off me

I liked him until
I discovered he
didn't like me
 - me me he didn't
like me

They said bad things
about me about me
no-one else me me
Said bad things about me

I hung myself
Me me I hung me...

TALKING IN BOXES

A man in a box
told me to watch my step.
A man in a box
told me to stop pissing around.
A man in a box
told me to shut my face.
A man in a box
told me to get it sorted.
A man in a box
told me I was a dead cert
for the big fire.
I went to confession yesterday...

EARLY IMPRESSIONS

Dad locked in
a room won't come out
sound of him laughing
wants to join a religious order.
Sister in another room
not talking to anyone
won't answer pretending
to read a book.
The doctor calls shouts
at her but she carries on
not reading.
Ambulance arrives takes
her away she leaves the book
by the side of the chair but
I am frightened to look at it...

THE GREAT HUMAN FARCE

I love you
I hate your guts
You're so kind
You're a cruel bastard
Shall we start a family
I'm having custody of the kids
You're so exciting
You're no fun anymore
Will you make love to me
Don't even touch me
I want to be with you
I've found somebody else
I really care about you
Drop dead!...

STRIVING FOR IMPERFECTION

Teach me to play the
game of life with all
its twisted rules.
Teach me positive thinking
that great human lie we
deceive ourselves with
in order to cope.
Help me to learn the
lie so I can survive too...

DIFFERENT KIND OF FATHER

My dad wanted
to be a priest
and my mum wanted
to be a house wife
and they fought like
cat and dog.
My dad called it
a pseudo marriage
- a con.
My mum called it
a disgrace.
They broke each other's
hearts and ours too
we buried them together...

STONE THROWING

Odd business that
throwing stones at one another
with intent to cause injury.
We don't do it any more of course.
There are more subtle ways of
hurting people.
I must have been thirteen
when I threw my last stone
in anger - I think I missed him...

PAUL

Remember how nice
it was to first be
called by your name
to hear it said,
especially by a friend.
Remember how nice it
was to first hear your
name - your own special
name and how important
you felt...

WIND UP

I was invited to dinner
by the vicar last week,
duck was mentioned.
I arrived on time with
a bottle of wine but he
did not answer the door.
I thought I saw the curtain move...

MY DOCTOR

I'm quite sweet on my doctor.
I gave her my book and invited
her to my reading.
(Needless to say, she didn't show up).
She has my medical records.
Why would she be interested in a
fat alcoholic predisposed to psychotic episodes?

PATRIOTIC WHITE YOUTH

Tattoos and flash wheels
nice little earners and thuggery
dodgy deals and racism
Cockneys make me sick.

Uncreative Unimaginative
money makes it tick
fancy clobber tedious slang
Cockneys make me sick.

Anti-trade unions subservient girlfriends
Individualistic - a mind of its own
except on the football terraces
Cockneys make me sick.

Loud mouthed show-offs won't be
ruled by Socialism, the cripple
beggar creed of Northern losers
Wheelchair politics is not for them
suntans and cash cards
Cockneys make me sick.

Big dicks and doing bird
keeping fit in case there's a war
bracelets medallions knives out
at the disco.

Oh! Come back stuka's all is forgiven
V2s and doodle-bugs do your stuff
rip the heart out this Capitalist monster
street by street like forty years ago.
Return and break their spirit once more
Cos cockneys make me sick.

DEATH

Death is a Socialist
he comes to us all
the rich the smug
the mad and the small...

The reaper's a lefty
a decent sort
he doesn't take
Barclaycard
he shits on us all...

He mocks our plans
causes much pain
arrives unannounced
in horrible forms...

Yet for all his faults
he ends suffering
for many and sorts out
the smart arses
once and for all...
I take my hat off to him,
death the greatest leveller
for sure...

THE SECRET CRIER

The old man wept
privately making
sure the windows
were closed and
mortise lock was
on the front door.
He had been caught
crying once before
in the trenches on
the Somme and had
been threatened
with a .38 revolver.

HORRIBLE THOUGHT

As I sat talking to the girl I loved
I noticed an axe on the fire-hearth
and a most unpleasant thought flashed
through my mind. It made me feel ashamed
guilty and rather horrible. I turned my
chair round so as not to see the axe but
it remained in my mind and I felt even
worse even more guilty that the axe had
such an effect on me it had caused me
to move my chair so I moved it back again.
'What's with all the chair movements', asked
my girlfriend. 'It's the axe isn't it?
I'll go and put it in the kitchen - out of
sight out of mind'.

NO SECONDS NO AFTERS

Oh cowardly humans
other animals can
accept death why can't
you. They don't go running
to church every five minutes
to listen to the deranged
prattle of some neurotic
vicar with a grotesque fear
of death. Just because you
can count to a hundred, write
the odd letter and still picture
your dead grandparents doesn't
mean you deserve to live forever.
Three score years and ten - say
it, say it instead of a prayer
and hold your head up high with
the other animals...

$C_2 H_5 OH$

One or two
I can't do
Three or Four
leads to more
Five or Six
I'm in a fix
Seven or Eight
lose a mate
Nine or Ten
never again
Anything over
nut-house in Dover...

HYPOCRITE

She said men are horrible -
they're sick they're violent
they start wars they kill easily
they're rough bullying domineering
tyrants, macho swines.
I agreed with her and said imagine
fancying one - how much sicker that would be
She slapped my face and left - collaborator...

MIRROR

Mirror Mirror
on the wall
why must I wear
this horrible colostomy bag...

Mirror Mirror
on the wall
explain the acne
on my face...

Mirror Mirror
on the wall
why the harelip
club foot and pissin' wheelchair...

EXPOSED

Trapped by his
semi-confessional
writings; was forced
into a role which
eventually killed him.
And for what? a few
miserable publications...

BRILLIANT STUDENT

Excelled in all subjects
a great sportsman
wonderful sense of humour
fell off a cliff...

Active in everything
lived life to the full
a generous nature
stabbed to death
at a disco...

A great guy
with a great future
cheerful and optimistic
head crushed in
a car crash...

Full of ideas
always dashing about
popular with the ladies
fell onto a javelin...

A kind heart
and sense of fairness
always fun to be with
inhaled his own vomit...

MAN TO MAN

She said she was getting
heavy phone calls and
wanted to borrow a man's
voice for the answer machine.
I volunteered immediately
but she said I'd be no good
on account of my stutter.

G.B.H.

I've pushed you off buildings
into trains and spikes
I've removed bits from
walls imagining your eyes
I've slashed pillows and
curtains butted doors
and shattered glass
I've done all this and more
Yet I still see you laughing
in a Glasgow bar...

THE LAVATORY ATTENDANT

I go to work
at my own convenience
angry and demoralised
sit on a stool
and dream of nice places...

In they trickle
coughing spitting
splashing about
I take out a book
but it doesn't help...

The smell is awful
the clients surly
can't bear to eat
my sandwich.
If only I'd passed
an exam or two
this job is hell...

There's sick on the floor
and a couple are screwing
in a cubicle I should really
say something but what's
the point.
This isn't a job it's
an insult...

5.30 the shitting
and pissing is over
time to lock up.
My clothes stink
and I just want to
get drunk...

UNHAPPY HOUR

I enter alone it is a
large pub and I go through
the nightly ritual of looking
in every room even though I
know I will recognise no one
the rest of the pub know this
too but I look anyway. Occasionally
I do see a familiar face but it
ignores me because it is frightened
of my loneliness so I pretend I
have forgotten those few lines
spoken when he or she was feeling
generous and skulk off to a quiet
corner thinking to myself it's
about time I left London...

NATURE POEM

This morning,
I observed from my bedroom window
two squirrels chasing each other -
from tree to tree they leapt but
it wasn't for my entertainment.
They had had a furious row which
had erupted into violence.
I suspect a woman may have been involved...

FIREMEN

Big fat sons of Satan
clumsy psychopaths
never on time...

Pathological liars
so full of hate
not a bit of compassion
never far from trouble...

Absolute cowards
obsessed with water
noisy buffoons
shouting about nothing ...

Bone-idle incompetents
children in uniform
can start nothing
can only put things out...

The most corrupt
profession in the world
A job for sneaky
little shits and
greedy egomaniacs...

THE LONELY RASPBERRY BLOWER

All on my own except
for a phone.
I ring at cheap rate
to unleash my hate.
It's a form of art
a telephone fart.
It gives them a fright
in the middle of the night.
When I feel mean
I'm especially obscene.
I go on till I yawn, quite often dawn.
Then I make a cup of tea
and wonder if they think
it's me...

GAMES WITH GRANMA

Sometimes when my Gran
was sleeping I would have
fun tying her shoelaces
together or placing objects
on her head. One time I removed
her left eye with a bayonet...

HURRY UP AND DIE

I wish more people
I know would die
I like a good funeral
and seldom cry.

How long must I
wait for them to die
I like a good drink and
a piece of pie.

BEST SELLER

Poetry doesn't normally sell,
but mine might because I intend
to embark on a series of bizarre
motiveless murders on and around
Hampstead Heath. Poetry doesn't
normally sell, but mine might...

SUDDEN REALISATION

And then it occurred to him
maybe he hadn't lived at all

and was chuffed....